# YOUNG HEARTS

*Inspirational Poetry
by children and young people with ME*

Foreword by Terry Waite

The Young ME Sufferers Trust

Published in the United Kingdom in 2004
by
The Young ME Sufferers Trust

ISBN 0-9548893-0-4

The moral rights of the authors of this work have been asserted by them in accordance with the Copyright, Designs and Patents Act 1993.

All rights reserved. No part of this publication may be reproduced, stored in a retrieval system, or transmitted in any form or by any means, electronic, mechanical, photocopying, recording or otherwise, without the prior permission of the copyright owners.

Copyright © 2004 The Young ME Sufferers Trust

The copyright in the individual contributions rests with the individual authors.

Editor
*Jane Colby FRSA*

Design and illustrations
*Kerry-Ann Edge BA (Hons)*

Printed and bound by Bookfile
Orbital Park  Ashford  Kent  TN24 0GA

Inspired by
and dedicated to the memory of
Jade Louise Scarrott
14 years

I struggle with a juggling act – recognising the value of things I can sometimes do, or used to be able to do, but striving to like and respect myself just as much when ME forces me to simply Be.

*Carli Barry*

I love to write poems. I write how I feel and what I'd like to do in the future. It helps to write down how you feel.

*Lauren Griffin*

# CONTENTS

| | | |
|---|---|---|
| TERRY WAITE | Foreword | 9 |
| VICTORIA FLUTE | On Hold | 10 |
| JANE COLBY | Who Wrote the Poems? | 11 |
| | | |
| JADE SCARROTT | Light What Light | 13 |
| ROBIN SANSOM | From Which To Climb | 14 |
| LESHIA M HOOK | The Abyss | 15 |
| HELEN DAVIES | I Feel | 16 |
| SHEENA HEWITT | I Am All Ages | 17 |
| CHLOE HALSTEAD | Flying Free | 18 |
| GILLIAN STEPHENSON | A Mother's Eye View | 19 |
| CATIE JENKINS | Please Don't | 20 |
| JACOB LOHSE | Cereal In A Glass | 21 |
| CLAIRE WADE | Cuddly Bear | 22 |
| RACHAEL MARSHALL | Old Bear | 23 |
| RACHAEL MARSHALL | A Poem For My Cat Snowy | 24 |
| TOMMY F ROBIN | Being In A Wheelchair | 25 |
| JAMES TILLEY | The Spider In My Room | 26 |
| VICTORIA WESTERN | The Roses | 27 |
| LINDA MCLEAN | Heather | 28 |
| JADE SCARROTT | China Doll | 30 |
| SHEENA HEWITT | Tears | 31 |
| KATIE ANNE EVANS | Year Of Hell | 32 |
| RACHAEL MARSHALL | My Hell | 33 |
| JADE SCARROTT | Shadows No Longer | 34 |
| JADE SCARROTT | Life's Wing | 36 |
| ROBIN SANSOM | Boundless | 37 |
| JADE SCARROTT | Forest Of Dreams | 38 |

| Rachael Marshall | Autumn Moon | 39 |
| Rachael Marshall | The Fairy Dance | 40 |
| Leshia M Hook | For You | 42 |
| Jade Scarrott | Like The Moon | 43 |
| Eleanor Ward | To Sleep | 44 |
| Jeanette Mills | So Go Sweet Child | 45 |
| Polly Maynard | Do You Ever Look Up | 46 |
| Jade Scarrott | With Feathers | 47 |
| Lucy Hayes | Secrets | 48 |
| Robin Sansom | Tears | 49 |
| Lois EJ Thorpe | When? | 50 |
| Rachel Goolden | My Window | 51 |
| Rachael Marshall | A Friend | 52 |
| Rachael Marshall | Memories | 53 |
| Jade Smith | Fame | 54 |
| Anna Sheppard | Reliving A Memory | 55 |
| Robin Sansom | Driftwood | 56 |
| Karen Hall | Your Jade | 57 |
| Jade Scarrott | Our Parents | 58 |
| Jade Scarrott | Who's Her? | 59 |
| Ana-Alicia Bryant | Different | 60 |
| Rachael Marshall | To Belong | 62 |
| Lois EJ Thorpe | Peace | 63 |
| Robin Sansom | Trust Can | 64 |
| Jessica Wilkinson | Loneliness | 65 |
| Alex Bacon | Is It Really ME? | 66 |
| Rachael Marshall | My ME | 67 |
| Sheena Hewitt | When I Talk | 68 |

| | | |
|---|---|---|
| Rachael Marshall | The Forgotton One | 69 |
| Anna Harwood | A Distant Girl | 70 |
| Heather McLean | You Don't Understand | 72 |
| Thomas Kendall | Humming Bird Eyes | 73 |
| Kirsty Hinton | Alone With ME | 74 |
| Sarah Humphrey | My Permanent Shadow | 75 |
| Amelia Edwards | Roller Coaster Ride | 76 |
| Rachael Marshall | Childhood Dream Clouds | 78 |
| Sarah Humphrey | Cloud | 79 |
| Jade Scarrott | Being | 80 |
| Katy Dunn | No More | 81 |
| Robin Sansom | Hanging Out In Bed | 82 |
| Emma Patrick | Dream Touched | 84 |
| Victoria Flute | My World's Stopped | 86 |
| Lucy Hayes | Getting There | 87 |
| Rachael Marshall | Autumn Is Here | 88 |
| Natalia Goldman | When You Are Forced | 89 |
| Robin Sansom | Faithful Wings | 90 |
| Sarah Humphrey | I Will Win | 91 |
| Katie From SA | I Said Goodbye... | 92 |
| Rachael Marshall | Winter Nigh | 94 |
| Sheena Hewitt | Skating | 95 |
| Jade Smith | Christmastide | 96 |
| Rachael Marshall | Christmas Tree | 97 |
| Rachael Marshall | Snow Falling | 98 |
| Rachael Marshall | The Winter Faerie | 99 |
| Kirsty Strain | Wings Of An Angel | 100 |

Myalgic Encephalomyelitis - The Illness     102
Hannah Gibson          Over The Rainbow     104

# Foreword

There are times when all of us will find it difficult to listen to the news on the radio or view it on TV. There are so many stories of suffering throughout the world that they become difficult to bear. Often we listen to them and we have to let them wash over us, otherwise the burden would become intolerable. It is when suffering hits us personally that we cannot put it to one side so easily.

Life is not fair and often we cannot understand it. Suffering comes to all of us but not in equal degree. Some certainly suffer more than others and through no fault of their own. All we can say with certainty is that so very often something creative can emerge from the deepest grief.

Suffering need not destroy. Jade had a short life with many difficulties. The end of her mortal life was tragic and yet her memory lives on in the poems that she wrote during the years she spent on this earth. She, along with many others in this book, demonstrate that out of suffering something creative can emerge. Jade's life on this earth was short. Her memory lives on as does her spirit seen in these poems.

May they bring hope and inspiration to all of us - especially to those who at this time feel the burden of suffering.

*Terry Waite CBE*

## ON HOLD

The cure you would like to have is currently unavailable. Please try again later.

The life you are trying to reach knows you are waiting. Please hold.

Your hopes are important to us - we will be with you shortly. Please hang on.

*Victoria Flute*

# Who Wrote The Poems?

For *Young Hearts* we have collected poetry and thoughts from children and young people with ME from the tender age of seven years.

Most of the contributors are in their early, mid or late teens, because this is when ME typically strikes. Most are registered with The Young ME Sufferers Trust. Their poems may span years of work, or be their first ever venture into verse. One young woman in her twenties joked: "Hope it's OK to send poems in now I'm old!"

Some contributors have several poems here, written over the course of their illness. ME can last years – and often does. Whatever the age of the author, the same themes recur: how to survive loneliness and isolation; the need for friends and support from family; the plea for others to understand; dreams of a brighter future; a world without pain.

Through all the trauma and sorrow, these poems speak with a universal voice – the voice of childhood and youth, coming to terms so early in life with the reality of serious illness, the harshness, but also the beauty, of our world.

Some of these poems moved us to tears. Others made us smile. Above all, we found them inspirational.

The world cannot but respect the integrity of these children's words. They fearlessly expose the raw struggle that living with ME represents. They describe the search for a way to attain peace of mind and hope through the dark times. They show how the quirky, the funny, the unusual, can provide light relief from the long endurance test that is ME.

Above all, they show us how – despite everything – to "hold that dream".

*Jane Colby FRSA*

# LIGHT WHAT LIGHT

Who is screaming all that pain?
Who's that girl I see?
What's that light at the end of the tunnel?
The light that seems so real.

Shouting, screaming, feeling,
Believing my fate
All the darkness covers my face.
It blinds me in fear
The thunder is my tears.

The room that's always locked
The key that's always lost
The soul that's trapped
The soul that lives in a cage
The happiness has faded
The strength has moved out
The pain has moved in.

A little girl screaming, screaming, screaming,
A little girl shouting, shouting, shouting
A little girl feeling, feeling, feeling
Someone is torturing her mind
Or should I say, some thing
That controls her life.

*Jade Scarrott*

# FROM WHICH TO CLIMB

It is a pit from which to climb
A muddy path full of holes
A name unknown but a weight it hangs
Weary are the blistered soles
Time does fly, the pile does grow
Memories fade, time is sold
Old dreams cry, pain takes hold
The mist of fear is icy cold
It is a place from which to see
A hidden cave full of strife
An end unsure but secrets found
There is more to this life
Time does fly but I exist
Here and now I raise a fist
Memories fade, dreams can die
But I'm alive – "alive!" I cry.
And while I live I have hope
A turning page in my book
It had its time but now I fly
And I'll take back all it took.

*Robin Sansom*

# THE ABYSS

I am so tired of this cold place
My heart slowly fades to stone
I am lost to where I truly belong
Terrified of all the unknown

I yearn to sleep so deeply
Until all the world fades away
And I can finally find some peace
In a reality that will not fray

A hand to grasp onto in the dark
That will never leave me cold
And pulls me back from the abyss
A light to forever hold

To know I could be rescued
From even the deepest of wells
By a singular hand of wisdom
To rise me from these hells

If the shadows take my soul tonight
And freeze me to my core
Reach out to me with blessed warmth
And help me again to soar

*Leshia M Hook*

# I FEEL

I feel like an old person who can't do things.
An old lady in a wheelchair who can't use all her
energy. Then has none at all.
I feel like an energy bean who takes a bath,
Then….
I feel like a tea bag being drained of all its energy.
I feel like my head is made of concrete
with a man drilling in it.
I feel like my legs are made of jelly,
they don't want to hold my body up any more.
I feel like my legs are just waiting to collapse.
I feel like a sponge full of water.
I feel like a balloon so when I pop, water comes out.
I feel?…..

*Helen Davies*

# I AM ALL AGES

I am all ages.
I am the child who disappeared,
passing like a shadow from your lives.
I am the one who gained knowledge,
understanding beyond my years.
I am in body what time made me,
yet in spirit I do not match.
I am a youth kept captive from society,
now underage for my circle.
I am someone who is old,
having learnt the true value of living.
I am myself and now alien to you.

*Sheena Hewitt*

# FLYING FREE

As I lie on my pillow
I sit up straight and lower my head
I see the birds on the breeze
And the sparrows in their trees
The leaves fallen on the floor
As I stand at the door
The birds perch on my hand
And I say "This is your land…"
And that's what happens as I lie in my bed
I sit up straight and lower my head

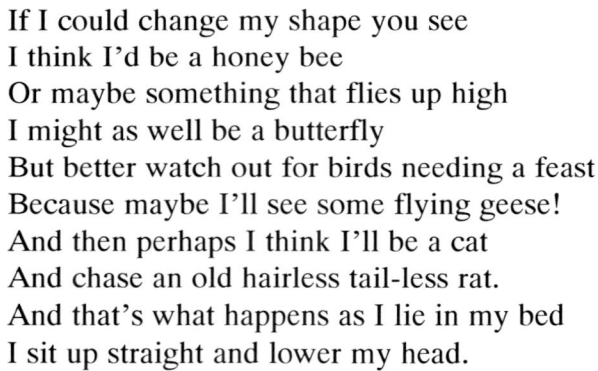

If I could change my shape you see
I think I'd be a honey bee
Or maybe something that flies up high
I might as well be a butterfly
But better watch out for birds needing a feast
Because maybe I'll see some flying geese!
And then perhaps I think I'll be a cat
And chase an old hairless tail-less rat.
And that's what happens as I lie in my bed
I sit up straight and lower my head.

As I walk along the sand
I realise that this is their land
I dive into the cool green sea
And see a dolphin and yes… it's me!
And then I meet a friendly shark
And hear the herald angels – hark!
The sun glistens through the sparkling waters
A dolphin jumps high and gives me hope.
As I lie back and think of these wonders
I sit up straight and lower my head.

*Chloe Halstead*

# A MOTHER'S EYE VIEW

My daughter dressed herself today
"That's very good" I hear you say
"If she is two, or nearly three."
She's thirteen – and she has ME.

Such small achievements now, our aims,
Not "top in maths" or "good at games"
For that's the way it has to be
When you are coping with ME.

Awake at night, in pain by day –
The world a million miles away
Adrift upon a choppy sea
That's caused and fuelled by ME.

Some friends have stayed, and those we treasure
Knowing friendship is life's greatest pleasure.
Others have flown: it had to be –
They couldn't cope with the ME.

And yet, there are some brighter times.
We laugh, and joke, and make up rhymes
And notice things that they don't see,
Who are not hampered by ME.

She's learned to smile to hide the tears,
Gained wisdom far beyond her years,
Learned patience and humility
From this cruel teacher called ME.

*Gillian Stephenson*

# PLEASE DON'T

Please don't tell me I look just fine,
Please don't say that I'll be right in no time
When I can hardly make it through the day.
You don't have to live this life
So please don't tell me you know what it feels like
Or how it really is to be this way.

Please don't tell me I'm just a little tired,
Don't shake your head and say I'm not really trying
When I want to spend some quiet time in bed.
"Come on, let's get you out the house,
We all have our ups and downs."
You haven't heard a single word I've said.

Potions, pills and wonder cures –
I don't believe in miracles.
I only wish you understood the truth,
That to watch and wait and pray,
Live in hope from day to day,
Is all that either one of us can do.

*Catie Jenkins*

# CEREAL IN A GLASS

I feel like an ass
I put cereal in a glass
My brain doesn't function right
Though I try with all my might
Memory used to be a doddle
I'm lucky now if I can waddle
All of my body aches
If I even pick up a supid rake
OH DEAR
I fear
I forgot the "t"
What's happening to me?
Oh yes
I see.
It's called M.E.

*Jacob Lohse*

# CUDDLY BEAR

Thank you for my cuddly bear
He's cute and soft with fluffy hair
I'll give him lots of loving care
So a big THANK YOU – love from
Claire
xxx

*Claire Wade*

*PS Claire called her bear Beefy and she says he made her day when he arrived.*

# OLD BEAR

All alone he sits on a chair
A poor lonely little old bear
Patched and frayed a torn ear and eye
He looks so unhappy as he starts to cry
His owner has left him he's all alone
With a paw to his eyes he lets out a moan.
Sad little bear sniffles and cries
Then rubs at his little black button eyes.
"I wish for a playmate for someone to love,"
Then startled he turns and looks up above.
Standing there is a little young girl
With big blue eyes and hair with a curl.
"Are you OK?" asks the girl to the bear
As she gently lifts him off the old chair.
"No" sniffs the bear "I've been left alone."
"Oh you poor little thing I'm taking you home."
She cuddles him close and kisses his head
"I'll love forever my little old ted."
So the bear is now happy his wish has come true
He has someone to love and play with him too.

*Rachael Marshall*

# A POEM FOR MY CAT SNOWY

Snowy is my black cat
He is beautiful
Though he is now quite fat
Now the weather's cool
At night he sleeps on my bed
He takes up all the space
Sleeping by my feet or head
Even by my face
His eyes are a bright yellow
He's got the loudest purr
He's such a sweet fellow
With his soft black cuddly fur
You see I love my Snowybug
More than anything
And that's why I love to kiss and hug
The wonderfulness that is him

*Rachael Marshall*

# BEING IN A WHEELCHAIR

Being in a wheelchair for ME is lots of fun
Being in a wheelchair for ME is like having a bun
I can mow down old ladies by the tonne
Cos being in a wheelchair for ME is lots of fun
Being in a wheelchair for ME is not hell
Because *I* can run as well.

*Tommy F Robin*

# THE SPIDER IN MY ROOM

He's gone in a crack.
I don't know when he's coming back.
Maybe he's lurking behind my wardrobe
trying to get out
But will I shout?
Maybe he's under my bed
trying to sneak up to my head.
He could be behind my desk
having a little rest.
Finally he shouts "Yippee I'm out."
I look at him
He's very thin
So I let him out the door.

*James Tilley*
*7 years old when bedbound with ME*

# THE ROSES

The roses stand
Tall and bright
Shining in the sunlight.
Smell the scent
Of the lovely flowers
Pink and red all pretty colours.
The bees come for food
While inside the flower moves
Pollen rubs upon his side, and so he
Spreads the pollen wide.

*Victoria Western*
*First published by Dome Vision in* Zoe's Win

# HEATHER

Locked
In a dark silent world
An eerie tomb
This was once
My daughter's room.

Dead
To the world
And all its joys
Dead to the music
And teenage toys
Dead to friends
Laughter and fun
Dead to family
….poor little one.

And yet....
There is life
A little thread
One that lets her
Lie in bed
She goes to the toilet
And eats her food
She would do much more
If only she could.

Yes.
There's a pulse
Dull thud of a heart
Beating in hope
Yet so torn apart
How do you live
Through a death such as this?
Do  butterflies come
From such chrysalis?

*Linda McLean*

# CHINA DOLL

Sat in the corner, she's unaware
Of danger that haunts her
That creeps up and hides her

She has no idea
Of the life that's around her
Sorrow that controls her
Through everything she does

Dusty she grows
And paler, fading rose
She comes to a stop
And with no life in her limbs she drops

Now to and fro
Her mind starts to fade
Her hearing isn't quite the same
It starts getting dark

She's lost all light
Until she's all a blank
No more listening
Or word of mouth

No more can she see
Move or feel
With a blank mind she lies
With nothing but her last memory

Of constant heartache and pain!

*Jade Scarrott*

# TEARS

Felt emotion
in those crystalline drops;
a moisture to denote
ones inner thoughts.

*Sheena Hewitt*

# YEAR OF HELL

Every day is the same
It's so bad I gave it a name
The year of hell is what it's called
It gets so dull and so bored

My friends don't know what it's like
To live in hell day and night
Knowing when tomorrow comes
It's so pointless and so dumb

Hoping it will go away
Overnight or in a day
My friends just left without a clue
My mum and dad'll pull me through

I have headaches and can't sleep
I can faint and land in a heap
They're so bad they drive me crazy
It makes my vision very hazy

Hoping it will go away
But it won't – it's here to stay
For the time I'll have to cope
But I'll never give up hope.

*Katie Anne Evans*

# MY HELL

This is my hell
I am alone
The inky blackness
An endless void
Cold invades
My heart encased
Like freezing ice
It traps me here
In dark and loneliness
Like death
Just me
My hell
My life.

*Rachael Marshall*

Shadows no longer scare me
Like they did before
But I now know there's no danger
Like there is outside my window

Glass cannot save me
Protect me from the world
Protect me from the illnesses
Or war or cold hearted fools

I beat myself trying
To understand this cruel place
Why we couldn't prevent this
This unlucky turn of events

Where all we wanted to do
Was create a better place
When all we ended up creating
Was heartache and pain

With lives we put in danger
Just to prove we're right
With tombstones we build and speeches
Like we're not ashamed to hide

Right for our conscience
So we can sleep at night
But it will never be right again
Not for every new born baby

Or for another's life!

*Jade Scarrott*

# LIFE'S WING

On the end of life's wing
On the end of its heart
On the end of its caring
On all it has touched
With feathers it's fluttered
With every heartbeat it soars
With every lover's first kiss
And every baby's first word
With every smile life takes
And with every tear it sheds
A story once told
Becomes more unknown
With lessons once learned
Now just ash and stone
And with every summer gone by
And with every memory long died
And with another dream dead
Our bird turns to cry

What has he now, no comfort, no warmth
No love to feed his hunger
No hope to quench his thirst
So with a broken wing he lies…

Please, hopeful bird, do not die!

*Jade Scarrott*

# BOUNDLESS

How can I express this restless passion that I hide ?
This fairground of spinning thoughts and feelings that I ride,
Spiraling down and shaking me up,
Through joy and pain, through fear and love,
Dancing dizzily round and round,
The words are lost and make no sound.

How can I make clear the reflection on the waves?
Fragmented and confused is the image it betrays,
Tossed about and broken up,
Deep, deep down and up above,
Searching for something that's me,
The sun goes down, I cannot see.

But deep within a spirit lives,
Above all sound, beyond all sight,
It rises up this time again,
And lifts me high above my pain,
Where I am still and free from hunger,
In perfect love, in awesome wonder,
On blazing wings my heart takes flight,
Beyond the boundaries of my mind.

*Robin Sansom*

# FOREST OF DREAMS

That forest full of dreams
Filled with silver and gold trees
With a sky glazed light blue
Blackbird feathered flight
Nesting eggs - counted five.
Five pints of water fill a puddle
Seventy-five hundred fill a river
Trees filled with magical fears and
Delicious apples – tasting them is forbidden.
Time is not something you will find, for
Time does not pass, it just stands still
Like a daffodil's bulb.
Forest animals, stunning creature sights
The soft silky touch of long white-coated grass
But try and linger, not one weed to count.
Beneath the feet of a golden haired deer
A path opens up that leads to a rainbow
Filled with desires.
There's no need to wish or even hope or dream
For what's there to wish for when you're in
The forest full of dreams?

    Time to tell you
    About that forest full of dreams…
    But what is there to tell?
    Have you not been listening?

*Jade Scarrott*

# AUTUMN MOON

I see the moon out the open door
In the sky of the deep dark velvet night
The frosty air that freezes breath
White mist that rises before the light
Bathing all in silver light it hides
Behind the wispy late autumn trees
The land sparkles in frosted night dew
Standing in the cold light of moonlight freeze

*Rachael Marshall*

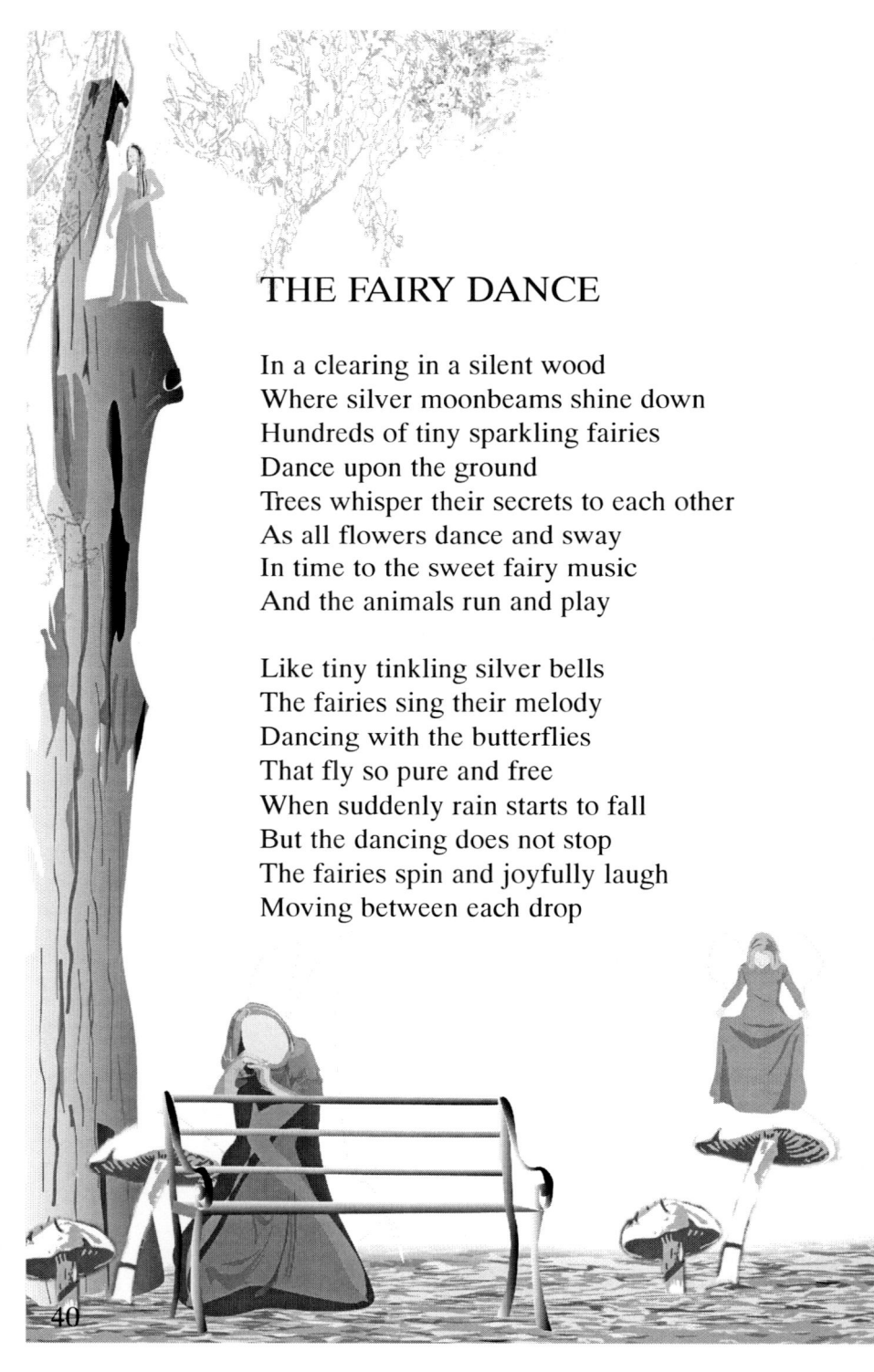

# THE FAIRY DANCE

In a clearing in a silent wood
Where silver moonbeams shine down
Hundreds of tiny sparkling fairies
Dance upon the ground
Trees whisper their secrets to each other
As all flowers dance and sway
In time to the sweet fairy music
And the animals run and play

Like tiny tinkling silver bells
The fairies sing their melody
Dancing with the butterflies
That fly so pure and free
When suddenly rain starts to fall
But the dancing does not stop
The fairies spin and joyfully laugh
Moving between each drop

Intertwining tiny hands and arms
Fresh flowers in their hair
Dresses of petals and spider web lace
Flow delicate and fair
Their cheeks a sparkled silver sheen
And with eyes so full of light
They turn and sway and jump and fly
In this beautiful shimmering night

*Rachael Marshall*

# FOR YOU

For you I'd sing a lullaby, to help you drift to sleep
And sing it to you as you rest, and watch as you choose dreams
    to keep

I would dream a dream for you, and fill it with pure light
To chase away all your fears and doubts, to give you strength
    to fight

If I was able to make your wishes come alive, I'd forsake my
    own for you
And draw out your deepest, brightest hope and pray for it to
    be true

If I could capture a shining star, take it from the dark sky's bed
I'd cradle it to sleep and give it to you, so your creativity and
    love is fed

I may not have the power, to bring the stars to you
But I will always be here, if you need a hand to hold onto

The stars bed may be far away, but your dreams do not live in
    the sky
Trust in your power of love and I will help you find where indeed
    they lie

The light that is inside of you, burns brighter than a star
Your dreams are just the beginning of what you really are

*Leshia M Hook*

# LIKE THE MOON

Like the moon
You start as a half
But then (like the moon)
It finds its meaning
(to be beautiful)
And becomes full – filled
Like you.

*Jade Scarrott*

# TO SLEEP

To sleep
as night's curtains close
and wipe the blackboard clean
Today's mistakes
drift idly by
destroyed by darkness here
We dream, we wish
to start anew
on shooting stars that fall
to wake to life
fresh and clean
pain gone
where once before
blankets ruffle
pillows crease
as people lie in rest
and thoughts leave us mortals
to a plane
where dreams are all that's left
The inevitable torture of the day
succumbs
to night's warm call
So I lie and dream
wait for the time
when daylight
rains and pours.

*Eleanor Ward*

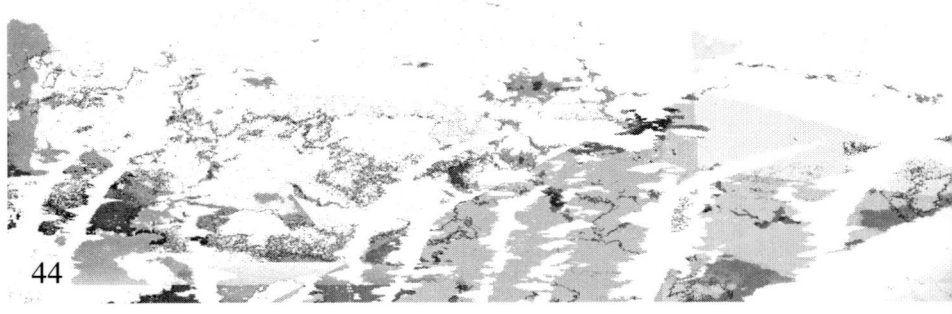

# SO GO SWEET CHILD

Falling in raindrops,
Against the summer sky,
Bringing its freshened air,
To where it's no longer dry.
Whispering drizzle,
Falling past trees,
As it travels softly,
In the gentle summer breeze.
So go sweet child,
Dream until you keep,
And listen to heaven's heartbeat,
Until you are asleep.

*Jeanette Mills*

# DO YOU EVER LOOK UP?

do you ever look up when the sunlight crests the dawn
and wonder where the night has gone
to see the sun rising to see a new day just begun,
but you not really sure what happened to yesterday
what happens when your life drifts without your guidance
you look behind and wonder what is this purpose of yours

    did you forget what you were dreaming what you knew you
        could become
    yesterdays are gone and you can't reclaim the past
    everyone's got their problems don't let them bring you down
    keep up-beat and smiling but don't be afraid to fall
    'cause people you trust will always be there when you trip.

    do you ever wonder if you'll ever be free
    chains that keep you grounded when all you want is to soar.
    you see the people flying, want to join them there
    but just hovering is hard and faith is slipping away.

    did you forget what you were dreaming what you knew you
        could become
    yesterdays are gone and you can't reclaim the past
    everyone's got their problems don't let them bring you down
    keep up-beat and smiling but don't be afraid to fall
    'cause people you trust will always be there when you trip.

*Polly Maynard*

# WITH FEATHERS

As a gentle breeze hovers
Above horrendous weather storms
Above the rains and the thunder
Above the sun and the stars

Above all in living and all in life
Even the heavens cannot reach this flight
Spirits that wander the circle of life
Spirits that control our dreams at night

Our feelings are a result
Of power from this point
Of circles and of squares
That moves us in our nightmares

Every first tear and every first smile
Every first laugh and every first mile
Every new beginning and every circle's end
Spirits rise unto the skies

And every heart that once belonged
Turns into a feather that can forever roam
Above all which will remain unknown

*Jade Scarrott*

# SECRET

In the hospital I hear people crying
Mostly babies
Sometimes mothers
At night-time me.

Hopelessly weeping
Tears seeping
Through ashamed fingers.

Head throbbing
Gently sobbing
Into a sympathetic pillow.

Fitfully crying
Limply lying
In a borrowed bed.

An intrusive torch
Flashes through my curtainless window
Beneath my blanket I shrink
Praying they do not know.

*Lucy Hayes*

# TEARS

Oh tears flow once again
Upon my cheeks of bareness
Wash them clean of all the pain
Of all the loss and all the shame

Wash my cheeks as white as snow
Fountains rise from down below
Release your streams of soothing balm
In waters deep restore the calm

Oh tears flow unashamed
Welling up from down below
Tears of hurt and tears of peace
But healing comes in the release

Oh tears flow without fears
Wash away the wasted years
Tears of joy and tears of sorrow
Reveal the hope of tomorrow

*Robin Sansom*

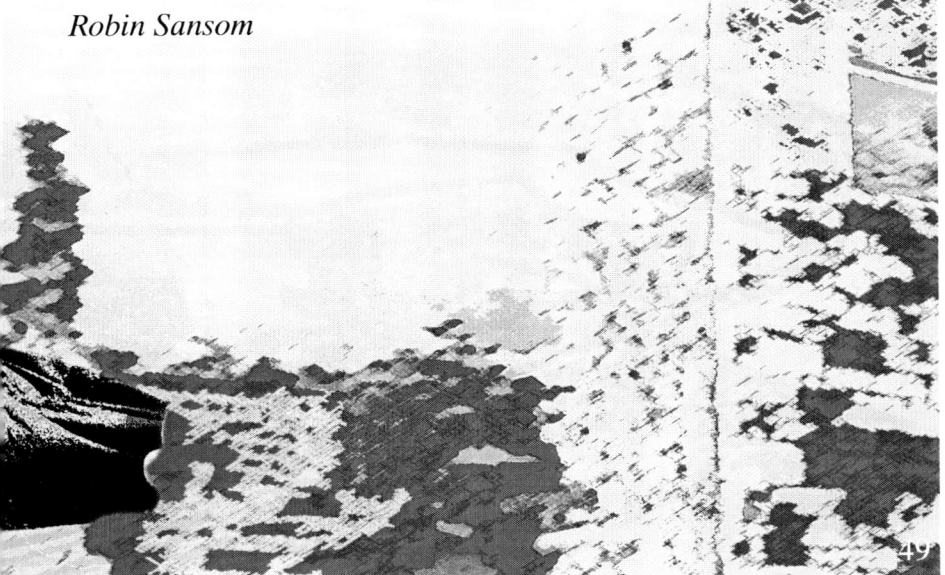

# WHEN?

I'll be back at school by September
Three weeks at the end of term won't hurt,
So I take the three weeks, only
They turn into three months.
September comes... and goes.
Now summer's dead, it's dark by four o'clock.
Those three weeks of sun and stillness seem three years ago.
I lie in bed watching the trees turn from green to gold to gone
And Christmas is all but here.
For weeks on end I've been indoors,
I'm fed up with stale air.
I spend the days lonely, on my own,
No one seems to care.
My friends have all forgotten
What it's like to see me in school.
I have too.
I've stopped making plans for "when I'm well".
When am I going to be better?

*Lois EJ Thorpe*

# MY WINDOW

Out of my window
I can sometimes see
Dancing white butterflies
And a waving willow tree

Out of my window
I can sometimes hear
Screaming, soaring swifts
And a pigeon cooing near

Out of my window
I can sometimes smell
The grass after rainfall
And the lavender I know well

Even behind closed curtains
I know they are there
And I dream of the day
We will meet without a care.

*Rachel Goolden*

# A FRIEND

A friend should be someone who's always there
Who no matter what happens will always care
And who'll pick you up when you are down
If your boyfriend dumps you will come around
Someone to help you through good times and bad
Someone to comfort you when you're sad
A friend to share with and listen to
And you'll be all of these things for them too
But a friend is not someone who when you're too ill to go out
Doesn't bother to call or come about
Or phone or text just to say hi
Who only lives round the corner so I don't know why
They haven't bothered to keep in contact with me
Cos I thought we were all best friends you see
But now you all seem to have forgotten me
It hurts - friends forever we said we'd always be

*Rachael Marshall*

# MEMORIES

Shining sun and bright blue skies
Happy laughs and joyful cries
As we play upon this green
Games of tag and kings and queens
We're carefree children full of fun
No worries for school is done
The summer holidays stretch ahead
Bike rides, beaches, late to bed
And ice creams from the ice-cream man
A special summer treat from Nan
To play in the park and climbing trees
Buying bouncy balls and penny sweeties
Getting up late and calling on friends
Playing in the fields and making dens
Eating ice-lollies which we all made
Drinking ice-cold lemonade
And these summer times are the best
A time to play and run and rest
And everyday we play together
In these holidays which last forever

*Rachael Marshall*

# FAME

Fame lasted a couple of Days
Now I'm glad it's gone away
No-one knew me before
Now I am known to a lot more
In my battle for people to Know about ME
I felt happiness inside of me.

In Days to come
Will I be remembered for my Bravery
or will I be forgotten quickly?
In my darkened room
I remember Days gone by
a bit of courage entered my life
hope it stays for the rest of my life.

I thought my Fame had gone away
but today landed on the middle page.
Couldn't believe the reaction I had
Some people were quite sad.
Nothing more I can say
Just hope others like myself
Find the courage to get through their Day.

*Jade Smith*

# RELIVING A MEMORY

I walk alone,
Treading the damp dewy grass.
My breath makes steamy patterns
In the cold crisp air.
Hands snug in pockets,
Only the sound of my rustling coat
The bare trees contrasting
Against the light blue sky.
And then I hear it,
The beautiful babbling of the stream.
I smile as I approach the bridge
Then, leaning on the railings
I watch the clear dancing water
Sparkling white in the winter sun.

*Anna Sheppard*

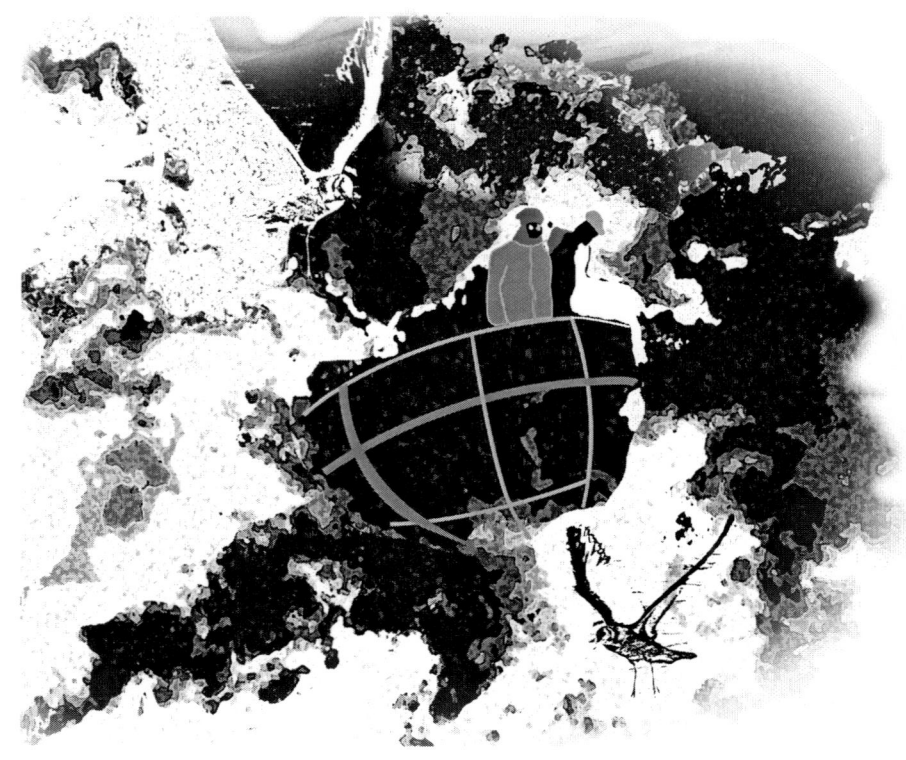

# DRIFTWOOD

The driftwood in the ocean
Twists and turns
In senseless direction
Up and down upon wave of emotion
Between two worlds
Dead wood afloat
Dark sky above
Deep sea below
Horizons blank
But stars above
Watching waiting hoping dreaming
For a distant shore to rise.

*Robin Sansom*

# YOUR JADE
*Dedicated to the Scarrott family*

your Jade was great
she was the best
from times I knew her
now let her rest.

she always smiled
no matter what
she cheered me up
I'll miss her a lot.

from toddler to teenager
perfect from head to feet
she enjoyed life
the nicest person you'll ever meet.

now she is in heaven
but her spirit won't fade
she's looking down on us
and she'll always be – your Jade.

*Karen Hall*
*Friend*

# OUR PARENTS
*A poem of love*

With hearts of gold
They both withhold
In each others' lives
They made their own
With each other's love
Support and life
They started as caterpillars
And bloomed into butterflies
And with each other's love they fly.

They gave us life
Love and a future
For when we look at them
We see heaven, hope and happiness
Like a flower they grow and bloom
In spirits, mind and word
With so much life and so much love
It brings us joy to know they're near us.

In all they do, in all they've done
From a past they started
To this present they are
And to the future a world
Of memories filled with love
With the sun as their flame
Which burns for them each day.

*Jade Scarrott*

# WHO'S HER?
*Especially for mummy*

Her eyes are sparkling green
Her smile is warm and friendly
Her hair is like sunshine
Her skin feels smooth yet soft

She looks like an angel
She moves like a god
She smells like flowers
Her voice is heavens above

Earrings and jewellery
Don't need to show her beauty
Kindness and caring
Is who "her" is.

    (whisper –
    it's you)

*Jade Scarrott
when 9*

# DIFFERENT

I always feel ill
I always feel left out
At school
When everyone's playing
And doing PE
There is me
Standing there with
My back brace
Everyone's looking
Whispering to each other
About me.

Why?

I'm no different to anyone else
I'm just ill.
It's not my fault if I have ME
Or a curved spine
Or asthma
Or I can't hear very well
Or I shake.

So I just want to say
To all those children who are like me...

Ignore them
You're the brave one
And just remember that!

*Ana-Alicia Bryant*

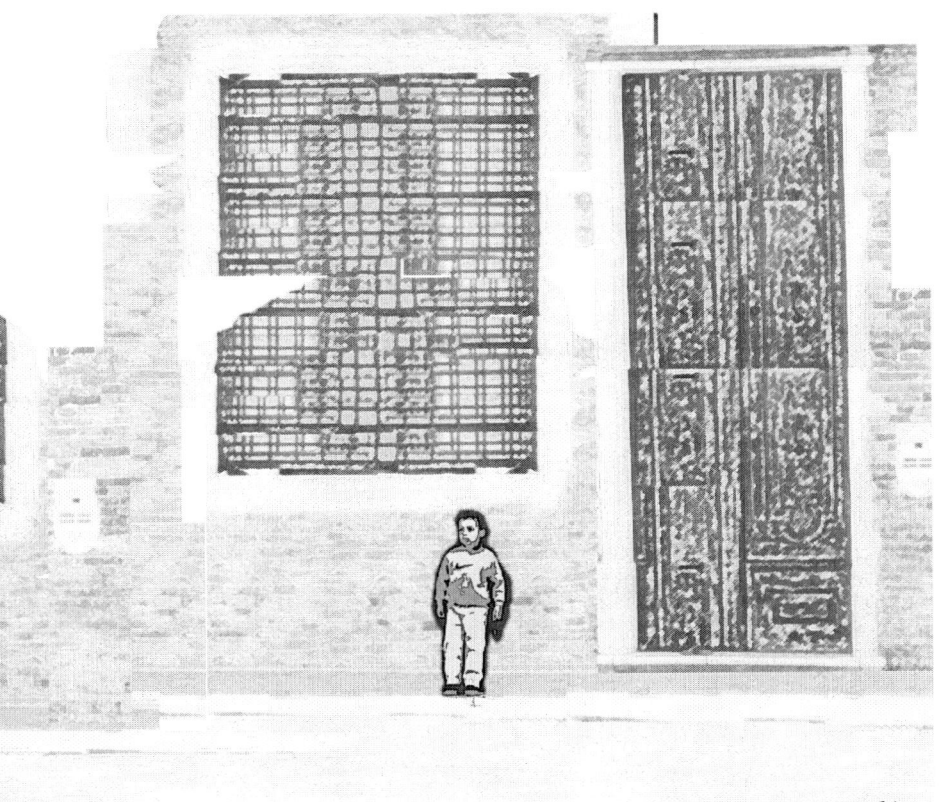

# TO BELONG

Where do I belong you ask
Hiding behind your hidden mask
Watching happy people all about
But why has your life not turned out
The way you had it all planned
What to do, who to be, it was grand
But now that doesn't belong
You don't and everything's wrong
How did you get here? What did you do?
Why do they fit in and not you?
Does everyone feel this way?
They don't look it, they never say
They have their groups have their friends
But you're on the outside at the end
So you walk with your sad lonely song
Just wishing that you could belong

*Rachael Marshall*

# PEACE

The ship is at anchor, becalmed in the port
The wild rough winds of the ocean can't touch here.
Moored in undisturbed, quiet waters
Serenely docked, waiting calmly,
Silence reigns, but for the gentle lapping
Of waves against the boat.
She is being renewed, rejuvenated
For her next trip into stormy waters
The wind will howl and waves crash on her decks
But she will not go down, she can't be beaten.
With strong determination
She crosses perilous waters
Arriving safely at the port
With none of her crew lost.
She may be battered and broken,
But never beaten.
That is all in the future though,
For now she lies blissfully quiet
In the tranquil waters of peacefulness.

*Lois EJ Thorpe*

# TRUST CAN

Trust can form a bridge over a chasm of great fear,
For you will not let me fall; your hand is always near.
Trust can keep on walking along a broken road,
For you wash my feet in love and share my heavy load.
Trust can keep on burning through a long cold night,
For you blaze amidst my dreams, and give me strength to fight.
Trust can climb a mountain when it seems all strength has gone.
For you shine upon my heart the valley that's beyond.

Trust can keep on waiting for another year,
For I know that you have promised to wipe off every tear.
Trust can break free from the chains of many lies,
For I know you hold the truth I can't see with my eyes.
Trust can find the path to a higher goal,
For when I lose myself you redirect my soul.
And trust is never easy; there are questions and there's strife,
But I'll put my trust in you and this trust will save my life.

*Robin Sansom*

# LONELINESS

I feel so alone,
In a world full of people.
I feel isolated,
Although I am surrounded.
I feel cut off,
Even when the channels are open.
I feel dark,
In a world full of light.
I feel lost,
In the places I know.
I feel like a stranger,
In my own home.
In a world full of people,
I feel so alone.

*Jessica Wilkinson*

# IS IT REALLY ME?

My diaphanous friends did not lend their support
But dissolved in a blink since no progress report.
My inner beauty was a memory, a haze,
It remains secreted from view and humanity's gaze.

I was alone in a room with no doors,
Ensnared and caged tightly within fatigue's jaws.
Confined to a house, my own private jail,
With little respite except sunshine and mail.

I languish in refuge, wrenching muscles do ache
Am I still diagnosed as a hoax, a good fake?
A fog cloud has loomed over brain for too long,
Blurring my vision, choking my song.

I have sought refuge in the small and inane,
Through relentless dark hours of dejection and pain.
A twinkling of light shatters silence and gloom –
Like a phoenix, I'll fly from the depths of my tomb.

*Alex Bacon*

# MY ME

Why do all these sounds seem so loud?
And my mind sometimes feel like a cotton wool
Why does my head hurt so very much?
And my skin sometimes feels tender to touch
Why do I feel weak like a floppy rag doll?
It's all eating away at my life like a black hole
I feel so tired and I can't concentrate
People think "missing school - that must be great!"
But it's not, you get lonely, people forget
And you feel left behind, trapped in a net
And people don't realise what it's like for us all
Living like this like our life is just stalled
You see that's why I write to comfort myself
That my life's not being wasted because of my health
One day I'll climb out of here and be free
And these will all just be my memories of M.E.

*Rachael Marshall*

# WHEN I TALK

Sometimes I think I may come across as being aloof,
maybe even I'm thought cold.
But you have to understand, caught by your conversation,
I answer awkwardly with no time to think.
My social graces are forgotten,
they were used a long time since.
For me it is difficult to reply to opening lines,
having talked little.
The skills are not yet relearnt;
so forgive my clumsiness,
make concessions,
and ignore my mistakes.

*Sheena Hewitt*

# THE FORGOTTEN ONE

Loneliness fills my life
I feel my heart encased in ice
Under all these watching eyes
Deep down inside something cries
All my hope and friends have gone
I am alone the forgotten one

Dark grey clouds rage inside
Obscuring light nowhere to hide
Tears fall down my tear stained face
All alone I have no place
But I don't want to be alone
Please take my hand and lead me home

*Rachael Marshall*

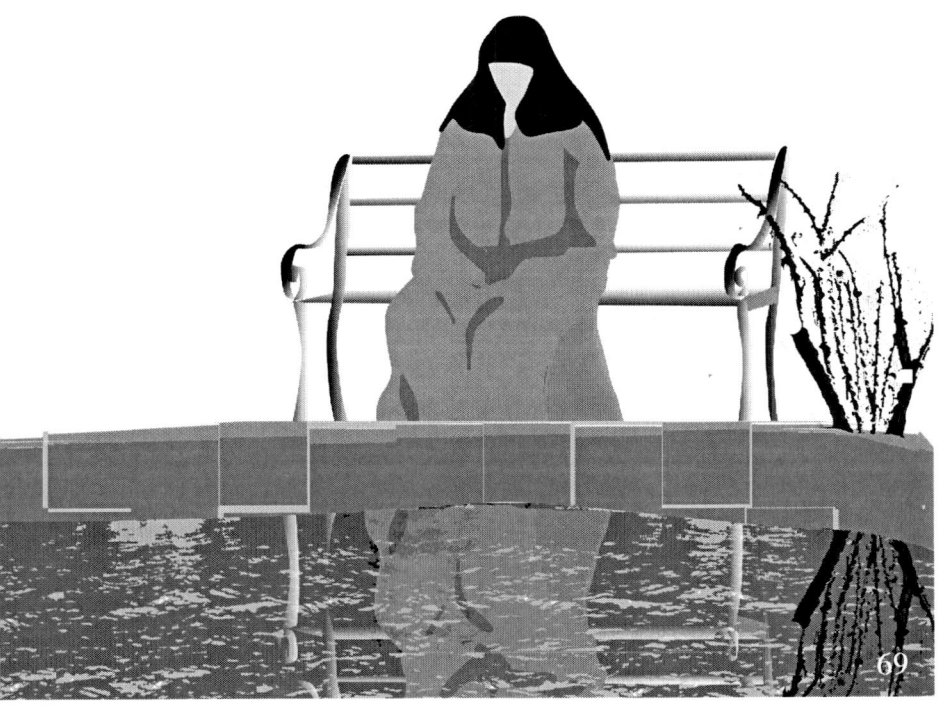

A distant girl lies back on plastic pillows clad with starchy linen.
She looks into space listening to the silence of the hubbub and
    commotion.
The smell of disinfectant spattered to shroud the grime lurks in
    the air
And mixes with the scent of overcooked dinners combined with
    stale, musty perfume.

Babies scream, reaching out for their mothers who sit worrying
    beside them
People rush in slow motion, the sound of their shoes leaving
    their bodies behind.
An agitated boy charges past knocking papers off walls, causing
    havoc in his track.
A gaggle of pubescent students follow an aging surgeon
    cowering behind his back.

Life rushes past her, every day seems the same, every day is the same.
Variation is an unknown word and affection is measured out in seconds.
The same song rings through her headphoned ears in a continuous monotone.
Thoughts mull over in her head, pondering, contemplating this stark existence.
White walls covered with pealing transfers reminiscent of the yesteryear.
In the distance a piercing wail is coupled with beeps of broken machines.
In this place it is quite easy to hide, to blend in with the surrounds.
Disturbed only to see how cold you are or how fast your heart pounds.

Everything has its time and place, time to eat and time to sleep.
Time to get dressed in a bathroom equipped with windows to peer in.
Time to talk when silence overcomes and time to be alone when you want to babble.
You wait for the times to come around, yet they disappear and you wait once again.

Night time comes and an orange glow illuminates the patterned curtains.
Earplugs muffle the tumult brought upon by equipment signalling complaint.
A distant girl shuts her eyes, chokes back her tears and embraces her desolation.
Rocks backwards and forwards, her loneliness fuelling her desperation.

*Anna Harwood*

# YOU DON'T UNDERSTAND

I tell you how I am
I try to explain as best I can
But you don't really see
How it's all affecting me.

I'm no longer who I used to be
Tired, alone and ill, that's not really me
I used to be laughing, happy, sporty and free
I do really want to act like I used to be.

There is no cure for this illness
So I have to survive through this poorness
And I know it's hard for you to keep in touch
But I really need you, Very Much.

*Heather McLean*

# NO MORE HUMMING BIRD EYES

No more humming bird
eyes for me
No more the feel
of the warm sun
on my face
whispering sweet
nothings
as I lie on
the ground.
I wish I was
trapped in your memory
as I was before
before all this.
How was I before?
It seems so long
now
and my memory is a
shotgun filled wall
disjointed and fragmented
with precious pieces
missing.

A fitting testament
to this illness
is that
there are
no more humming bird eyes
for me.

*Thomas Kendall*

# ALONE WITH ME

I try to think to myself
What's it like?
It's a bit like a shadow
It's strong and then it fades.

You try to run
And you try to hide
But it reappears.

And when it's gone
You know it is still there
It follows you everywhere.

Is it part of me?
Does it belong to me?
Like a shadow.

*Kirsty Hinton*

# MY PERMANENT SHADOW

You're there with me every day and night
Never letting go!
You hurt me as much as you can
The pain becomes unbearable
You've made your way into every corner of my body
Refusing to let go.
I cry and cry, this pain is getting too intense,
Yet you hurt me even more.
I've nowhere to run or even hide
As you've become my permanent shadow
I beg you, dear God, please help me escape
                      this pain that I'm in
Please let me escape the shadow that haunts me!

*Sarah Humphrey*

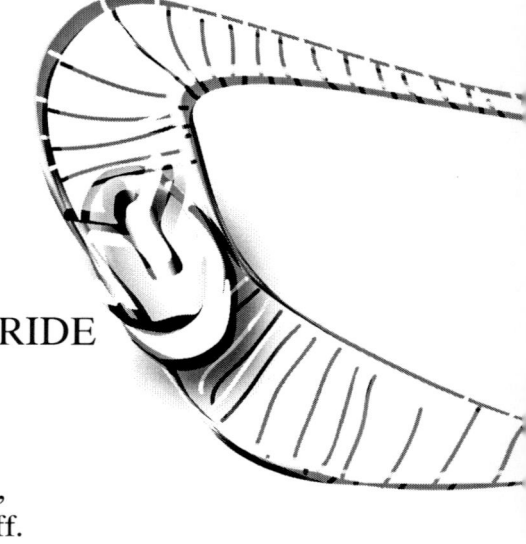

# ROLLER COASTER RIDE

It's the Journey of M.E.,
The dreaded roller coaster
Which innocent people desire,
But once on there's no way off.

We climb the steep hill of optimism,
The hope of soon returned good health.
Plummet to the depths of energy,
Leaving us helpless and exhausted.
Too spent to do more.

Then the loop of a brief respite,
Carrying us up on the wings of anticipation.
Experiences new and novel.
But in a flash it's over,
Back to pain and despair.

We approach the black hole,
The valley of depression.
Our insides seem to freeze,
A weight is dragging us down.

It's dark all around us.
Nothing to see except blackness.
No hope of deliverance,
Gradually we're slowing down.
Always to be stuck inside?

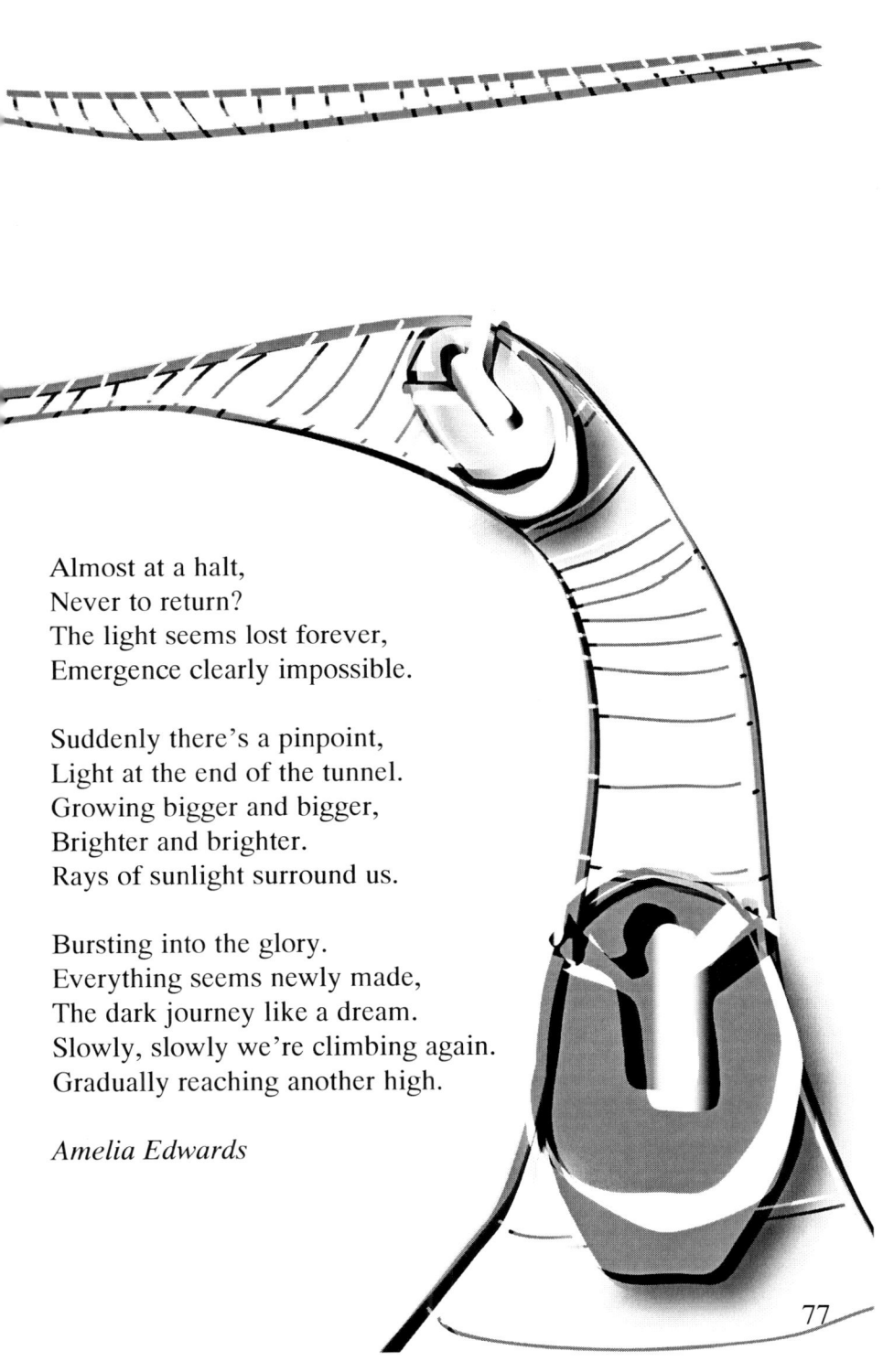

Almost at a halt,
Never to return?
The light seems lost forever,
Emergence clearly impossible.

Suddenly there's a pinpoint,
Light at the end of the tunnel.
Growing bigger and bigger,
Brighter and brighter.
Rays of sunlight surround us.

Bursting into the glory.
Everything seems newly made,
The dark journey like a dream.
Slowly, slowly we're climbing again.
Gradually reaching another high.

*Amelia Edwards*

## CHILDHOOD DREAM CLOUDS

Watching the clouds in the sky
Reminds me of childhood days gone by
Where every cloud became a dream
Of fairy princesses and castles a-gleam
Shining gold palaces of angels bright
In the giant clouds edged in sunlight
The pure white fluffy ones in skies bright blue
All different shapes maybe a dragon or two
My favourite were the evening clouds pink and gold
Full of fairy worlds where magic unfolds
The scary grey storm clouds always made
Me think of bad monsters - I was afraid
But on the other magical clouds away I flew
My dreams they always felt so true
But now those childhood days have gone
The memories left like a half forgotten song

*Rachael Marshall*

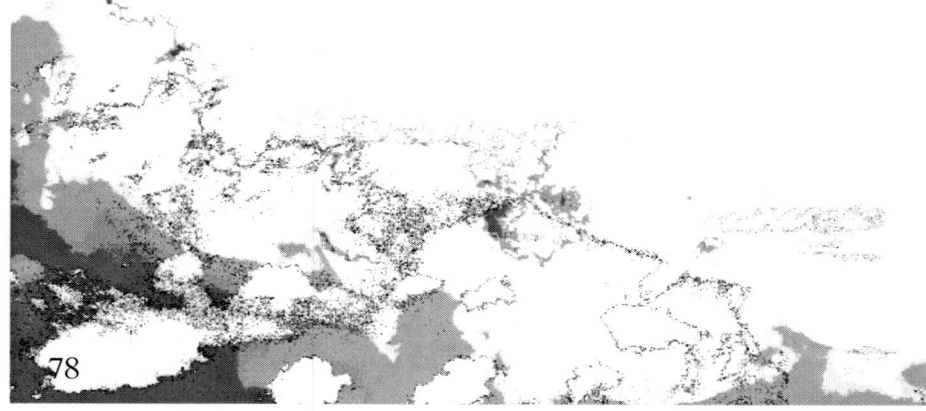

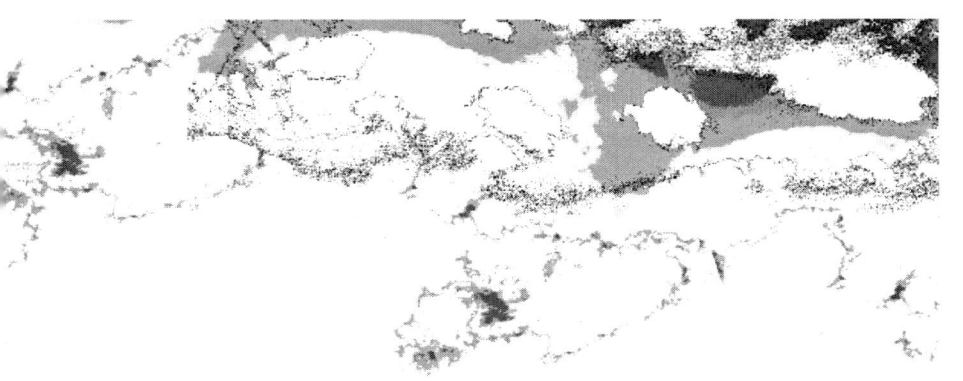

# CLOUD

Oh, how I wish I was a cloud
To be able to go wherever I pleased,
To be free and happy
To travel and to see.
Oh, cloud, you look so soft, like candy floss
We would let the wind blow us
           wherever we may please.
Oh, cloud, how I wish.
But it is just a wish?!

*Sarah Humphrey*

# BEING

With images in my head
With whispers in my ear
With uncontrollable emotions
Running through my skin

With nowhere to hide
And nowhere to run
I feel a shivering sting
All around me living

Being what I am
Losing who I was
Turning into hate
Losing all love

With courage all gone
And hope lost
With nothing left to wish for
My dreams turn to dust
Life is a mystery
That is surely true
We have no way of knowing
What is right from wrong?

What is perfect and what is incorrect
What is living and what is death
What's behind feeling?
And what's behind fight

Our wishes we shout out into the night
To whom we don't know is listening
Maybe someone we can't fight!

*Jade Scarrott*

# NO MORE

There's darkness lurking
That no-one can see
It sits locking its
Claws onto me
Draining strength and spirit.

Light surrounds it
And comforts me
It fights and battles
With the demon
Never giving up
Yet never winning.

The monster will tire
And light will grow
Stronger
And I will be refreshed
Energy seeping into
Every pore
The shadow will be dispersed
Gone and no more.

*Katy Dunn*

# HANGING OUT IN BED

Hanging out in bed, staring at the ceiling
A pain in my head, numbs all the feeling
Minutes merge with hours, the clock ticks away
Trying to remember the name of the day.

Some thought me lucky, staying home all day
Thought I was a yuppie, lots of time to play
But would they wear my shoes if they could really see
The bars on my window, my cry to be free ?

Hanging out in bed, sick of lying still
I went to the doc, he had no wonder pill
What did I do to deserve this crushing fall?
The sound of my cry echoes on the wall.

Some thought me lucky, lots of time to spend
But would they feel so lucky praying for a friend?
A soul to share the pain, of years trod in dirt
Would they wear the shoes, filled with thorns of hurt?

Hanging out in bed, longing for a cure
Body feels like lead, stomach is a sewer
My instinct is to fight, I push myself to crawl
Again I feel the bite as I hit the brick wall

Some thought me strange, I rarely was around
They just didn't see me writhing on the ground
Some didn't care, just went on their way
They had their own lives, had no time to stay

Hanging out in bed, chained by fatigue
Battery has gone dead, strength just a dream
Mountains I have climbed to fall in a pit
But the spirit borne within me says "I never quit".

*Robin Sansom*

# DREAM TOUCHED

Now I realise and understand
Why you never gave up, and
Even though life appeared to slip by
You rarely resigned it to being bland
Dreams were what you treasured
Held always close to heart
And even though the words of some
Shot through as painfully as a dart

You hoped, you dreamed
You gave, you loved
You were everything
You could and should have been

Life without you fades away
I wish you could have rested a little longer
Long enough to stay
I wonder - would it ever, could it ever
Have been long enough to stay?
I did so want to spend more time

So now I'll dream for you
In your loving memory
Hold close to mind and heart
The way you used to be
I'll dream the way your heart did
The way you did so much
Although I may never completely fulfil
I'll never leave a dream untouched

*Dedicated to all those who know that having M.E. takes away a part of "me" ~ keep hoping & dreaming.*

*Emma Patrick*

# MY WORLD'S STOPPED

In the rain I'll go dancing
      So I can feel the drops once again.
Into the wind I shall fly
      Delighting in its blustering sigh.
Jumping in a drift of snow
      I'll savour tingles in finger, toe.
Now, though, I must lie in bed –
      And watch all of nature's show instead.

I see larks singing way up high,
      Clouds floating across the big blue sky.
Sunsets, rainbows so vivid in hue,
      Each spring-new life so green, fresh and new.
Squirrels leaping through the trees,
      Autumn leaves twirling with each breeze.
My world's stopped, but life goes on –
      And I've time to drink in each new dawn.

*Victoria Flute*

# GETTING THERE

I can't believe where I am
Is it safe to believe?
How steady is the ground
I'm standing on now?

Look where I was
I've come such a long way
How did I get here
So quickly?

I am not there yet
I am here.
Am I?
I think so.

No, I'm sure.
I think.
No, I am
I'm here.

But I'm not there.
Yet.
I'll get there.
Soon.

*Lucy Hayes*

# AUTUMN IS HERE

Autumn has started it's easy to tell,
The cool fresh breeze a wonderful smell,
So crisp in the air on a frosty morn,
Crunchy leaves on the frozen lawn,
A refreshing change from hot humid days,
The chilling breeze and light autumn rays,
The leaves are falling as trees start to shed,
Burnished golds and sunset reds,
A thousand gold fairies dance through the streets,
Twirling down in colourful sheets,
Shorter days and longer nights,
Cosy and snug all wrapped up tight,
Bonfires lighting up the skies,
Like billowing smoky clouds up high,
The smell, the sound, the warmth, the light,
A comfort in the cold still night.

*Rachael Marshall*

When you are forced to contend
with both more and less
you dream, feel, you see this world
in all its terrible, trivial
glorious intensity.
And ultimately come to feel
blessed in knowing how to live
rather than exist.

*Natalia Goldman*

# FAITHFUL WINGS

Pale green leaves of a withered tree
Reach for light but thirst for more,
An aching heart for a spirit free,
The glimpse of love I found before.

The waves upon the open sea
Up and down like joy and pain,
The wind that whispers truth to me,
A glimpse of love from where it came.

A rising hope on faithful wings
Dares to fly into the storm,
A distant land, a dream that sings
Calls to me on this new dawn.

*Robin Sansom*

# I WILL WIN

I cannot see it.
Yet I feel it, every day surging through my veins
Like a swarm of a black plague
Clouding me, taking me, devouring me.
Where do I run?
Where can I hide?
As it always knows where to find me!
It stings, stabs me with pain, so constant
my eyes begin to water.
Every day my life is this
Knowing that it will attack me once again.
Will I beat it?
OF COURSE I WILL!!

*Sarah Humphrey*

# I SAID GOODBYE...

It was an overcast Monday morning. I sat on the bed and watched clouds roll over the dark crest of the mountain, visible above the garden trees in their glory of summer green. Time would not stop any more than would the ever-moving clouds.

In rooms down the passage, words from different mouths ran into and over one another, bustling in my ears. The smell of the house, sweet like the air from a cupboard long unopened, filled my nose.

I tried to decipher how I felt about my impending departure from this beloved place. Feelings, and words to describe them, chased around my mind.

I was tempted to believe that what I saw then, I would never see equalled, much less surpassed in beauty. I even doubted whether the next world or any other planet could hold such splendour. Unsure of what to do, I resolved to quietly watch the view from the window; as I did so, I noticed that every leaf, every twig and tree is a miracle of design. Trees grow and twist their branches into wonderfully pleasing lines. Leaves know which shade of green to acquire, so no two greens are quite the same. I looked up to the mountain. How could I succumb to bitter grief when the mountain was watching me? How could I insult its beauty by dissolving into sadness? How could I allow tears to blind me from the magnificence of nature? I couldn't.

Finally, these thoughts brought me to my senses. This was not the last time I would see that place. I would visit again. I got up and said goodbye.

*Katie from South Africa*
*After my first holiday away from home since falling ill.*

# WINTER NIGH

The silent night of winter dark
Frosty breeze and wispy trees
The ebony of shadow lies
Against the silver of snowy slope
From enchanted burnished moonbeams bright
Pools of rippling liquid silver shine
As stars shimmer in deep velvet sky
In the stillness of this winter nigh

*Rachael Marshall*

# SKATING

I want my mind to be
as clear as spring water.
Satisfy my craving;
an ice rink for my thoughts.

*Sheena Hewitt*

# CHRISTMASTIDE

Christmas is near,
Eyes filled with Tears
Can't tell people my fears
Wishing it be over,
Perhaps I can cope
Better next Year.

The thoughts of opening the Gifts
Which take Energy just to lift.
Time drags watching films.
Mealtime affects you more,
Family keep asking if you want more.

Christmas Tree lights shine Bright.
Decorations sparkle in the light.
I remember Houses decorated with lights.
Going to friends Boxing Night.
I try to remember things in the past
Patches of memory that don't last.

*Jade Smith*

Christmas tree all sparkly and bright
Windows warm with candle-light
Decorating every space
With holly, mistletoe, ribbons and lace
Presents lying round the tree
What's in them we'll have to wait and see
In every house that festive feeling
Of giving, sharing and receiving
Crackers, glasses, forks and knives
Waiting while the food arrives
Turkey, stuffing, mmm so good
Mince pies, cream and Christmas pud
Delicious smells everywhere
Christmas dinner made with care
Stockings hanging on the door
Full of prezzies and much more
With presents, laughter, food and wine
Oh Christmas is the BESTEST time

*Rachael Marshall*

# SNOW FALLING

Snow falling all around
Silent stillness not one sound
Nothing stirs this perfect white
Which sparkles in the early light
A soft pure blanket covers all
Delicate snowflakes softly fall
To cover grass, tree and hill
The frozen earth where time stands still
So beautiful untouched and new
A frosty white pearly hue
As far as the human eye can see
A sleepy calm of mystery
Its snowy beauty touches me
Its stark but pure reality
It shrouds the land in shimmering white
Whether it be day or night
And all around is encased
In a soft enchanted twinkling place

*Rachael Marshall*

# THE WINTER FAERIE

The winter faerie dressed in white
Like a snow flake dances bright
The spider lends his silver lace
To weave the magic to encase
The land in frost and ice and snow
And freezing winds that blow and blow

With her wand she patterns panes
Of windows, doors and weather vanes
Patterns of beauty, so delicate
Woven ice so intricate
Transparent wings and snow white skin
Ice blue eyes, mysterious grin

She flutters and dances all around
Her tiny feet frost the ground
Sparkling, twinkling, magical
The land is made so beautiful
By the winter faerie white
Through morning, evening, day and night

*Rachael Marshall*

# WINGS OF AN ANGEL

As I lie here in the silence
Listening to the peacefulness
I am suddenly aware of the changes
That are taking place within me.
I feel a cool breeze wash over me
And a bright light pass through.
What happens next takes my breath away
And that's why I'm telling you.

As I sit with the memories
Of who I am and what has been
I am suddenly aware of the changes
That are taking place within me.

As I sit and look at days gone by
I am growing the eyes of an angel.
And as I sing these words aloud
I am growing the voice of an angel.
As I feel the pain
The sorrow and the joy of what has been
I am growing the heart of an angel.
And as I take hold of what is to come
I am growing the soul of an angel.

It has all become so clear
That now I understand.
The heart of despair has passed
And I can see at last.

As I lift my head and give thanks
I am growing the faith of an angel.
And as I take my place in this world
As I turn and face my future
I am growing the peace of an angel.

When I turn and take a long
Hard look at myself
I notice that I have grown the wings of an angel.

*Kirsty Strain*

# Myalgic Encephalomyelitis – The Illness

Myalgic Encephalomyelitis (ME) is the biggest cause of long term sickness absence from school. It is a serious, potentially severe and chronic neurological illness, once called atypical polio. Viruses are known to be involved and it commonly occurs in clusters.

The name Chronic Fatigue Syndrome (CFS) is also used but is medically acknowledged as a "heterogeneous" condition *ie* there may be different types of illness within this overall term, which is also criticised for not conveying the severity of the symptoms and disabilities. The Department of Health refers to CFS/ME.

*World Health Organisation* neurological *classification of ME and CFS : ICD 10 G93.3*

## SYMPTOMS

*Brain and central nervous system*

Loss of memory, concentration, balance, co-ordination and fine motor skills
Difficulty sequencing words and numbers, speaking, thinking and absorbing information
Abnormalities of sensation (*eg* pins and needles, numbness) vision, hearing, sleep rhythm, temperature control, appetite, digestion, blood pressure, circulation, hormone production, response to stress
Development of sensitivities (*eg* to light, sound, touch, certain foods, chemical substances including perfume, paint, medication and anaesthesia)
Bouts of racing pulse (tachycardia) or skipped heartbeats and breathlessness
Mood swings, panic, anxiety or depression; these may result from brain dysfunction and the distress of misunderstood illness

*Generalised pain and weakness*

Pain in muscles, joints, head, back, limbs, chest and stomach
Muscular weakness and twitching

*Exhaustion coming on up to 72 hours after effort*

Even minimal exertion (cognitive or physical) can trigger exhaustion; the latent period after effort, together with the delayed reaction, is a classic sign of ME
Temporary hyperactivity may occur, due to brain dysfunction, resulting in exhaustion
Physiotherapists should beware of exacerbating the illness

**IS THERE A CURE?**

There is no straight "cure" for ME. The body needs energy to heal, so personal energy management is a helpful way to live with ME to encourage healing and avoid relapse. The Chief Medical Officer's Working Group on CFS/ME found that most children and young people with this illness will need a period of home tuition and/or distance learning, on a short or longer-term basis according to need (Department of Health 2002).

If treated inappropriately, ME can become much worse. In extreme cases, children can suffer fits or collapse. Some go through periods of partial paralysis and may need to be fed with liquids, through a tube.

Good old-fashioned convalescence is a good starting point, followed by careful management of life and education to avoid the downturns associated with trying to force the pace of recovery.

Further information at **www.tymestrust.org**

The Young ME Sufferers Trust
PO Box 4347 Stock
Ingatestone CM4 9TE

# OVER THE RAINBOW

Being ill helps me to appreciate the small things in life
like the honeysuckle that grows
and leaves a beautiful fragrance.

And so I will take one day as it comes
until I am flying over the rainbow
where I so dearly would love to be.

*Hannah Gibson*

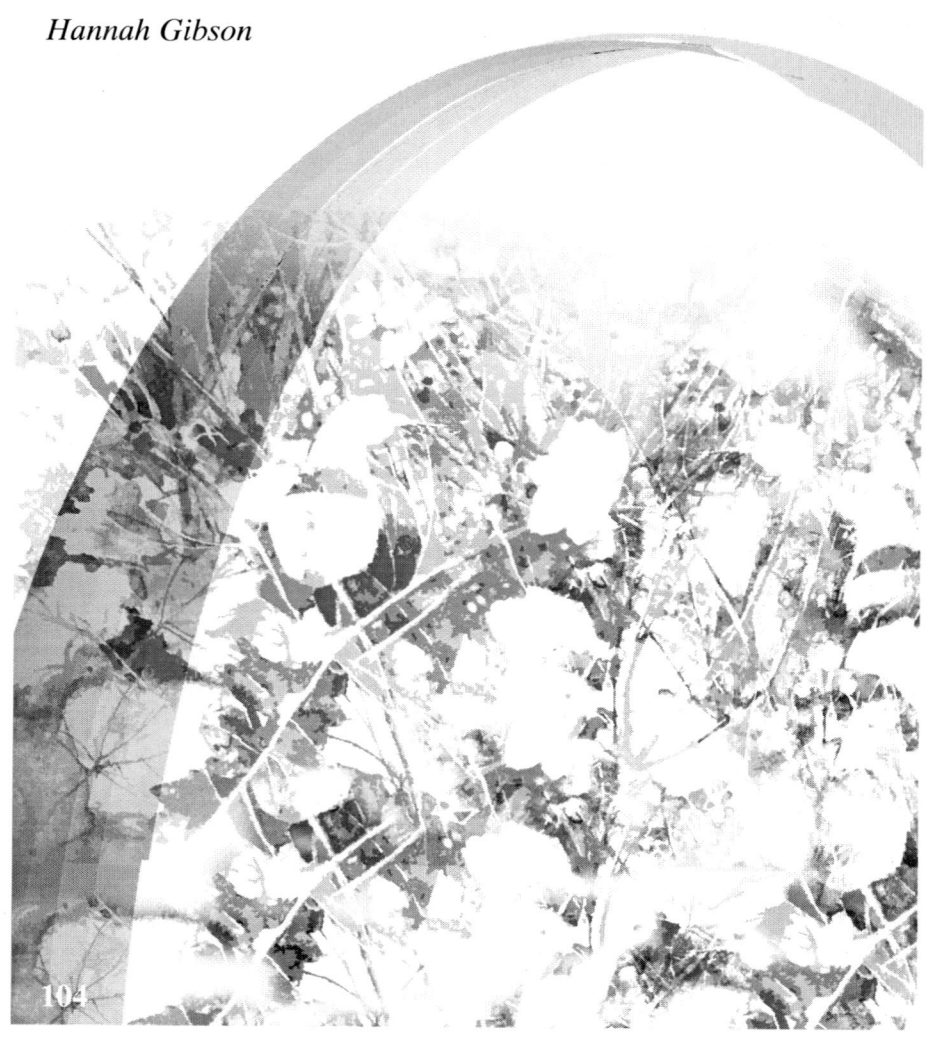